WHAT
EVERY
CHRISTIAN
SHOULD
KNOW

WHAT EVERY CHRISTIAN SHOULD KNOW

STUDY GUIDE

10 CORE BELIEFS
FOR STANDING STRONG IN A SHIFTING WORLD

DR. ROBERT JEFFRESS

BakerBooks

a division of Baker Publishing Group
Grand Rapids, Michigan

Published by Baker Books
a division of Baker Publishing Group
PO Box 6287, Grand Rapids, MI 49516-6287
www.bakerbooks.com

Printed in the United States of America

Library of Congress Cataloging-in-Publication Data
Names: Jeffress, Robert, 1955– author.
Title: What every Christian should know study guide : 10 core beliefs for standing strong in a shifting world / Dr. Robert Jeffress.
Description: Grand Rapids, MI : Baker Books, a division of Baker Publishing Group, [2023] | Identifiers: LCCN 2022018518 | ISBN 9781540903099 (paperback) | ISBN 9781493440986 (ebook)
Subjects: LCSH: Theology, Doctrinal—Popular works—Textbooks.
Classification: LCC BT77 .J34753 2023 | DDC 230.09—dc23/eng/20220624
LC record available at https://lccn.loc.gov/2022018518

Portions of this text have been adapted from *What Every Christian Should Know: 10 Core Beliefs for Standing Strong in a Shifting World* (Grand Rapids: Baker Books, 2023).

Published in association with Yates & Yates, www.yates2.com.

Baker Publishing Group publications use paper produced from sustainable forestry practices and post-consumer waste whenever possible.

23   24   25   26   27   28   29   7   6   5   4   3   2   1

CONTENTS

INTRODUCTION AND TIPS FOR STUDY GROUPS

Before beginning your personal or group study of *What Every Christian Should Know: 10 Core Beliefs for Standing Strong in a Shifting World*, please take time to read these introductory comments.

If you are working through the study on your own, you may want to adapt certain sections (for example, the icebreakers) and record your responses to the questions in this study guide or, if preferred, in a separate notebook. You might find it more enriching or motivating to study with a partner with whom you can share answers or insights.

If you are leading a group, you may want to ask group members to read one chapter from the *What Every Christian Should Know* book and work through the corresponding questions in this study guide before each meeting. This isn't always easy for busy adults, so encourage group members with occasional phone calls, emails, or texts between meetings. Help group members manage their time by pointing out that they can cover a few pages each day. Also encourage them to identify a regular time of the day or week they can devote to the study. They, too, may write their responses to the questions in this study guide or in a separate notebook.

Each session in this study guide includes the following features:

- **Session Topic**—a brief statement summarizing the session.
- **Icebreakers**—activities to help group members get better acquainted with the session topic and/or with one another.
- **Group Discovery Questions**—questions to encourage group participation or individual discovery.
- **Personal Application Questions**—an aid to applying the knowledge gained through study to personal living. (Note: these are important questions for group members to answer for themselves, even if they do not wish to discuss their responses in the meeting.)
- **Optional Activities**—supplemental applications that will enhance the study.
- **Prayer Focus**—suggestions for turning learning into prayer.
- **Assignment**—activities or preparation to complete prior to the next session.

Here are a few tips that can help you more effectively lead small group studies:

1. *Pray for each group member during the week.* Ask the Lord to help you create an open atmosphere where everyone will feel free to share with one another.
2. *Ensure each group member has the* What Every Christian Should Know *book and study guide.* Encourage each group member to bring his or her book, study guide, a pen or pencil, and a Bible to each session. This study is based on the New American Standard Bible (1995), but it is good to have several Bible translations on hand for purposes of comparison.

3. *Start and end on time.* This is especially important for the first meeting because it will set the pattern for the rest of the sessions.
4. *Begin each study session with prayer.* Ask the Holy Spirit to open hearts and minds and to give understanding so that truth will be applied.
5. *Involve everyone in the group discussion.* As learners, we retain some of what we hear and see, but we remember much more of what we hear, see, and do.
6. *Promote a relaxed environment.* If the group is meeting in person, arrange the chairs in a circle or semicircle. This allows eye contact among members and encourages dynamic discussion. Be relaxed in your attitude and manner, and be willing to share with the group.

1

GOD'S WORD

Session Topic: Does the Bible really claim to be God's Word? How can it be God's Word if it was written by human beings? Can we trust the Bible's claims and promises? This chapter will unlock truths about the Bible that will guide you in studying and growing from God's Word.

Icebreakers (Choose One)

1. If you could ask God any question about the Bible, what would you ask Him and why?

2. Select a few volunteers to play the telephone game—one person whispers a message to the second person, who whispers it to the third person, and so forth to the end of the line. How did the final message differ from the original one? What are some things you could do to ensure the message stays consistent when communicated from person to person?

Group Discovery Questions

1. Discuss the author's statement: "The answers the Bible provides are not only important but, for every person in the entire world, they are literally the difference between life and death." Do you agree or disagree? Explain your answer.

2. The author describes the Bible as "the basis of every theological claim in the structure of Christianity." In what ways does the Bible support every other Christian belief?

3. Read 2 Timothy 3:16. What do you learn from this verse about Scripture and its power to work in our lives?

4. Read 2 Peter 1:21. What does this verse reveal about how fallible people were able to produce an infallible Bible?

5. Which of the four evidences of the Bible's trustworthiness described in this chapter (dates of New Testament books, earliest reactions to the message, fulfilled prophecies, and archaeological discoveries) do you think is the strongest and why?

6. There are at least sixty-one prophecies in the Old Testament concerning the expected Messiah that were fulfilled by Jesus Christ. Read the following verses and discuss what these prophecies reveal about Jesus: Micah 5:2, Isaiah 7:14, Psalm 22:16, and Isaiah 53:9. What did you learn from this chapter about the significance of Jesus fulfilling all sixty-one biblical prophecies of the Messiah?

7. Read Hebrews 4:12. According to this verse, what makes the Bible different from other historical documents?

Personal Application Questions

1. Why does theology matter? And what real difference does it make in your life today? What do you hope to gain from your study of this book? Be as specific as you can.

2. Do you think Christians tend to view the Bible primarily as a source of knowledge, a source of personal transformation, or both? How do you tend to view it? Explain your answer.

3. Look up the word *inerrant* in a dictionary and write the definition in the space provided. Why do you think it is important that the Bible is inerrant?

4. Read Psalm 32:8 and Psalm 119:105. What do these verses teach about the Bible's ability to guide us? In what ways have you experienced the transforming power of Scripture in your own life?

5. The author stated, "God can lead believers today through prayer, circumstances, wise counsel, and even our desires." Have you ever been led by God in one of these ways? How did that guidance line up with Scripture?

6. Read Jeremiah 1:12. What encouragement does this verse give you regarding things in your life that seem to be out of control?

7. The wisest thing you can do is commit to studying the Bible and applying its wisdom to your life. What does your current study of the Word look like (e.g., time of day, place, method of study)? In what ways would you like to deepen your study of Scripture? Be as specific as you can.

Optional Activities

1. Break into small groups and ask group members to share the various ways they study the Bible. (Ideas include Bible apps on smartphones, podcasts, study guides, devotionals, and so forth.) What ideas can you implement in your own personal study of the Bible?

2. Make a specific plan to study your Bible this week, and ask someone to hold you accountable.

Prayer Focus

Thank God for giving us His Word, which is the basis of all Christian beliefs and filled with truths that change lives. Ask Him to reveal truths to you and use His Word like a scalpel to heal you. Commit to studying His Word regularly.

Assignment

1. Memorize Isaiah 40:8: "The grass withers, the flower fades, but the word of our God stands forever."

2. Read chapter 2 of the *What Every Christian Should Know* book and work through the corresponding study.

2

GOD THE FATHER

Session Topic: How has God revealed Himself to us? What does it mean that He is holy, all-powerful, and immanent? How can we communicate with Him? This chapter will explore the character of God the Father and help you strengthen your relationship with Him.

Icebreakers (Choose One)

1. Choose two people in the group to pretend they are meeting for the first time. How would they make themselves known to someone who knew nothing about them? Consider how their introductions compare to the ways God reveals Himself to us.

2. Break the group into two teams. Hand each team a sheet of paper with the name of a celebrity at the top, and give the teams two minutes to write down everything that comes to mind when they read that name. Which team had the longer list? How does this exercise illustrate the importance of names?

Group Discovery Questions

1. Read Psalm 8:3–4, Psalm 19:1–2, and Romans 1:20. In what ways has God revealed Himself in creation? Discuss specific examples.

2. What are some things we can learn from the Bible about God's character and His design for us?

3. How did God reveal Himself through the person and ministry of Jesus Christ? How does God reveal Himself through the Holy Spirit?

4. In this chapter, the author discussed ten attributes of God: *holy, just, loving, eternal, omnipotent, omniscient, immanent, transcendent, sovereign,* and *unchanging.* Which of these ten attributes is most meaningful to you and why?

5. What are some different names people use to refer to you? Why are those names and nicknames significant to you? What do they reveal about your relationships? What do God's names reveal about His relationship to us?

6. Choose one of the names of God discussed in this chapter. (See Genesis 22:14, Exodus 15:26, Judges 6:24, Psalm 23:1, and Jeremiah 23:6 for some ideas.) Share a time in your life or the life of someone you know when God lived up to that name.

7. What did you learn in this chapter about God's perfect plan to restore humanity's relationship with Him and give us eternal life? Briefly summarize God's plan in your own words. With whom can you share this message this week?

Personal Application Questions

1. Describe a time when God revealed Himself to you through Scripture. How did that experience affect your relationship with Him?

2. Consider the author's statement: "The Holy Spirit makes Himself known through our consciences. When we make decisions that please Him, He triggers in us a sense of connection with Him. . . . Likewise, when we make decisions that displease Him or pursue a path that leads us astray, He pricks our consciences. Working at a soul-deep level, the Holy Spirit lets us know that things aren't right." Describe a time when the Holy Spirit pricked your conscience about something. Did you realize at the time it was the Holy Spirit? How did you respond?

3. Read Psalm 34:8. In essence, God says, "Here's who I am. Come and see for yourself." Is your knowledge of God based on what others say about Him, or have you taken time to get to know Him personally?

4. In what areas of your life do you need God's wisdom right now? Read James 1:5 to discover God's promise to you about the wisdom you need.

5. If someone asked you, "What is God like?" how would you respond? Consider the attributes of God you learned about in this chapter, as well as other attributes of God revealed in Scripture.

6. Read 1 Kings 19:11–13. How did God choose to reveal Himself to Elijah? Sometimes God's presence is big, bold, and dramatic—and sometimes it is as personal as a whisper. Have you ever heard God's "whisper" in your life? What can you do to hear His voice more clearly?

7. What will you do this week to respond to God's invitation to get to know Him better? Be specific.

Optional Activities

1. Look up the names of God in the following verses and discuss (or write out in the space provided) what these names reveal about God: Genesis 22:14, Exodus 15:26, Exodus 17:15, Judges 6:24, Psalm 23:1, Jeremiah 23:6, and Ezekiel 48:35.

2. Break into groups of two or three and discuss this question: What are some things that hinder or distract you from pursuing intimacy with God? Come up with ideas to overcome these hindrances and pray for one another, asking God to help group members nurture a deeper relationship with Him.

Prayer Focus

Thank God for who He is. Praise Him for the attributes you learned about Him in this chapter. Thank God for revealing Himself to you and inviting you to draw on His wisdom. Ask God to continue to reveal more of Himself to you as you seek Him.

Assignment

1. Start keeping a prayer journal in a notebook or electronic file. Write down your experiences with God this week, recording the evidence of Him you see in the world around you. Record your prayer requests and God's answers. Share your answered prayers with the group in future meetings.

2. Read chapter 3 of the *What Every Christian Should Know* book and work through the corresponding study.

3

GOD THE SON

Session Topic: What did Jesus do before He came to earth? How did He reveal the nature of God? Why is it important that He experienced the same kinds of temptation, conflict, and suffering we do? This chapter answers difficult questions about Jesus's life, teachings, sacrifice, and return.

Icebreakers (Choose One)

1. During the past three years, what accomplishments or changes have you experienced in your life? What would you like to accomplish or change in the next three years? How does that compare to the three years in which Jesus changed the world?

2. Imagine you were to ask people around the world, including Americans, "Who do you think Jesus is?" What are some of the views about Jesus you think you would hear?

Group Discovery Questions

1. Describe various ways people celebrate the birth of Jesus at Christmas. Why is it important for us to remember that Christmas celebrates only Jesus's birth in human form, not the beginning of His life, since Jesus is eternal?

2. Read John 1:1–5, 14, and 17. What did you learn from this chapter about the significance of *logos*, the Word (or Word of the Lord)?

3. In the incarnation, "Jesus obediently and willingly laid aside His rights to come to earth and dwell among us." Discuss some of the things Jesus gave up when He willingly left heaven to live as a human.

4. Virtually everything we know about Jesus occurred during the last three years of His life. What are some of the things the Bible tells us about Jesus's ministry during those three

years? Read John 21:25 to learn what one of Jesus's biographers said about His life.

5. What expectations did the religious leaders of Jesus's day have about the coming Messiah? What expectations do people have of Jesus today?

6. Discuss the author's statement: "Jesus brought the law of Moses to a close by fulfilling every bit of it. It was the surprise ending virtually no one saw coming." Why is it significant that Jesus came to fulfill the law, not to abolish it? (See Matthew 5:17.) How did Jesus's sacrificial death negate the need for any further sacrifices?

7. Read 2 Corinthians 5:21. What spiritual transaction took place on the cross? To understand the personal nature of this transaction, replace the words "our"/"us" and "we" in this verse with your own name.

Personal Application Questions

1. Consider the author's statement: "If we're not careful, we can get lulled into believing we have a pretty good handle on who Jesus is and where He belongs in our lives. We decide which of His teachings are applicable and which ones might raise eyebrows. We think there are some things Jesus can change and some things He can't. We place our own expectations on the Great Defier of expectations." What expectations have you placed on Jesus? Is there anything you think Jesus can't (or won't) do? Explain your answer.

2. Read Hebrews 4:14–16. Why is it significant that, during His life on earth, Jesus was tempted and suffered as we do? What comfort does this give you about the struggles you may be experiencing?

3. The author said, "The impact we have on others' lives, in showing them Christ's love, begins with three simple words: *I see you.*" Describe a time when someone showed Christ's love to you. How did that affect you? Whom has God placed in your life for you to notice and demonstrate Christ's love to?

4. Read Luke 5:16 and Mark 1:35–37. What do you learn about Jesus's quiet times? How can you apply this in your own life?

5. This chapter examined Jesus's three priorities during His three-year ministry: *His Father's Word, His Father's presence,* and *His Father's will.* How can you prioritize these things in your life as well? In which area do you most need to improve? Be as specific as you can.

6. Read Paul's description of Jesus Christ in Colossians 1:15–20. Then consider this question from the author: "If Jesus Christ is sufficient to create and sustain the universe, to deliver us from the power of death, and to restore our relationship with God, don't you think He's sufficient to entrust with our lives?" Is there any area of your life that you don't think Jesus Christ can handle? How does this Bible passage affect your perspective on that issue?

7. According to Philippians 3:20, where is your citizenship, as a Christian? How could remembering your true citizenship affect your perspective on the things of this world and change the way you go about your life this week? Be specific.

Optional Activities

1. Make a list of the things the world considers valuable. Then read Philippians 3:7–11. How does understanding Jesus Christ and cultivating a relationship with Him help you put these things in proper perspective?

2. Sing or listen to a Christian song or hymn focused on Jesus Christ, such as "Jesus, Name Above All Names," "Jesus Paid It All," or "In Christ Alone." Use this time to worship Jesus and thank Him for what He has done for you.

Prayer Focus

Thank Jesus for obediently and willingly laying aside His rights to come to earth and dwell among us. Praise Him for choosing to suffer so He can be our faithful High Priest and being obedient to death on a cross so He would be our Savior. Confess any expectations you have placed on Jesus, and ask Him to reveal more of Himself to you as you seek to know Him better through prayer and God's Word.

Assignment

1. Memorize 2 Corinthians 5:21: "He made Him who knew no sin to be sin on our behalf, so that we might become the righteousness of God in Him."

2. Read chapter 4 of the *What Every Christian Should Know* book and work through the corresponding study.

4

GOD THE HOLY SPIRIT

Session Topic: What does it mean that the Holy Spirit dwells in believers? How can we grow the fruit of the Spirit in our lives? What are some of the spiritual gifts the Holy Spirit has given us? This chapter reveals the extraordinary things the Holy Spirit can do in and through us, if we allow Him to.

Icebreakers (Choose One)

1. This chapter discusses the "rule of three"—many music groups have three members, books and screenplays often feature a trio of characters, interior designers arrange items in groups of three, and so on. Discuss some examples of this "rule of three." In these groups of three, does one member of the trio tend to recede slightly? If so, which one is it?

2. Set up chairs and other items as obstacles in a maze pattern in the room. Choose two volunteers. Blindfold one volunteer and ask him or her to navigate the maze by listening to the guiding voice of the other volunteer. How is this exercise like listening to the Holy Spirit guiding us through life's obstacles?

Group Discovery Questions

1. In the teaching at most Christian churches today, do you think the Holy Spirit tends to be overemphasized, underemphasized, or about equal to the other members of the Trinity? Explain your answer.

2. In your own words, describe the role of the Holy Spirit in a Christian's life.

3. Describe a situation in which you required the Holy Spirit's assistance. What happened when you drew on His power? How can you become more purposeful about drawing on the Holy Spirit's power in your daily life?

4. In the Old Testament, leaders were "anointed and empowered by the Holy Spirit to fulfill [their] God-given calling to govern the people of Israel." Read Judges 3:9–10, Judges 6:34, 1 Samuel 16:13, and 2 Chronicles 20:14–15. What

phrase is repeated in these verses? What were these leaders empowered to do?

5. Discuss the author's statement: "Today, the Holy Spirit indwells every believer, fully and permanently, the moment we are saved. He will not depart from us. We cannot lose Him." Why is it essential to understand that the Holy Spirit will never leave a Christian? What comfort does this truth give us?

6. Read John 14:16–17, John 14:25–26, John 15:26–27, and John 16:7–11. What did Jesus teach in these passages about the presence and role of the Holy Spirit in the lives of believers?

7. According to 1 Corinthians 12:4–11, when we're born again into the family of God, the Holy Spirit gives each of us a spiritual gift, which is "both a desire and a unique power to be a part of God's ministry." What spiritual gifts are listed in this passage? (See also Romans 12:6–8 and Ephesians 4:11–12.) Which of these spiritual gifts can you observe in your fellow group members?

Personal Reflection Questions

1. Consider the author's statement: "Unfortuantely, far too many Christians go through life unaware of the great, supernatural power of the Holy Spirit within them. But the Holy Spirit is there, whether we choose to access His power or not. The Holy Spirit takes up residence within every person who accepts Christ as Savior." If you're a Christian, are you aware of the power of the Holy Spirit within you? Why or why not?

2. Read Ephesians 4:30. What do you think it means to grieve the Holy Spirit? (For a few examples, read v. 31.) Are you doing anything right now, in attitude or actions, that grieves the Holy Spirit? If so, confess your sin to God in prayer and ask Him to forgive you and help you in that area.

3. Consider the author's statement: "Anytime we feel pangs of guilt or regret—anytime we sin and feel the need to ask God for forgiveness—we know that the Holy Spirit is at work." Have you ever felt those pangs of guilt or regret? How did you respond? What happens when you ignore those feelings?

4. According to Romans 8:26–27, how does the Holy Spirit help you when you pray? Have you ever experienced this?

5. According to 1 Corinthians 2:11, what does the Holy Spirit know? Based on what you learned in this chapter, how does the Holy Spirit reveal that knowledge to you and other believers?

6. Read Ephesians 1:13–14. How did the apostle Paul describe the way the Holy Spirit secures your future?

7. What does it mean to be "filled with the Spirit"? The author described four main conduits by which Christians receive the Spirit's filling: *the Bible, prayer, the church,* and *obedience to God.* Has there been a time when you've felt energized through one of these conduits? Describe what happened.

Optional Activities

1. Read Galatians 5:22–23 and write out "the fruit of the Spirit" listed in these verses. Discuss how Christians can demonstrate each of these characteristics in our daily lives.

2. The author described worry as a "Spirit-quencher." Write down one or more things you are fearful about right now. Then ask God to help you confront those fears and give you the peace of the Holy Spirit.

Prayer Focus

Thank God for sending the Holy Spirit to indwell you at the moment of your salvation and to be your Helper, Comforter, and Guide. Confess any area of your life that may be grieving the Holy Spirit. Ask Him to help you respond to the Spirit's leading and access the Spirit's power in your life.

Assignment

1. Write out Galatians 5:25 on a piece of paper or sticky note: "If we live by the Spirit, let us also walk by the Spirit." Put this verse somewhere you will see it every day this week (such as your computer or car dashboard) to help you remember to listen for and follow the Holy Spirit's guidance.

2. Read chapter 5 of the *What Every Christian Should Know* book and work through the corresponding study.

5

ANGELS AND DEMONS

Session Topic: What are angels, and what role do they play in God's plan? What strategies does Satan use against us? How can we defend ourselves against demonic forces? This chapter shines a light on the spiritual battle raging all around us and provides a battle plan for defeating our invisible enemy.

Icebreakers (Choose One)

1. Set a timer for two minutes, and ask group members to write down as many things as they can that include the word *angel* or *angels*, such as movies, television shows, books, products, sports teams, cities, and so on. Why do you think our culture is fascinated by angels?

2. How are angels usually portrayed in television and movies? How are demons typically portrayed? Discuss specific examples.

Group Discovery Questions

1. Read Ephesians 6:12. According to this verse, what role does the spiritual realm play in this world?

2. Do you tend to think of angels and demons as "somewhere out there"? Discuss the author's statement: "The battlefield isn't just on our doorstep—it's also *within* us. This titanic spiritual war against the invading armies of darkness and wickedness takes place every minute of every day of our lives."

3. Should we worship angels? Why or why not? Read Revelation 22:8–9, and write what you learn.

4. According to Hebrews 1:14, what is the role of angels? Whom do they help?

5. Read the following verses and discuss what you learn about angels: Psalm 103:20, Psalm 148:2, Luke 15:10, and Hebrews 13:2.

6. According to the author, "Behind every false god in the world today is a very real demonic power. . . . An even more insidious way that demons lead unbelievers astray is by subtly tweaking aspects of the true gospel." What does 1 John 4:1 command us to do regarding these demon-inspired teachings? Discuss some examples of false prophets who lead people astray by promoting false religions or tweaking the true gospel.

7. Can Christians be possessed by demons? Read Ephesians 1:13 and discuss what you learn about who "possesses" Christians.

Personal Application Questions

1. Are you struggling with a frustrating boss, an uncaring mate, a rebellious child, or another difficult relationship or situation? What perspective does Ephesians 6:12 give you about that personal struggle?

2. Hebrews 1:14 says that angels are "sent out to render service for the sake of those who will inherit salvation." Can you think of a time that this might have happened to you or to someone you know?

3. The Bible says angels *sustain and encourage believers, reveal God's will to us, protect us from physical and spiritual harm,* and *minister to us in death.* For which of these four areas are you the most grateful? What comfort can you draw from knowing that the angels minister to you in these ways?

4. Consider the author's statement: "Have you ever felt an inexplicable weight of oppression you just can't shake? Have you ever been in an argument that turned hostile for no apparent

reason? Have you ever had a productive day suddenly derailed by a debilitating anxiety attack or faced a temptation that seemed custom-designed to entrap you? If you answered yes to any of these questions, then you've likely experienced demonic work in your life—just perhaps not in the way you expected." Can you think of a personal experience similar to these examples? Describe what happened. Did you realize at the time that it could be a spiritual attack?

5. Are you holding back anything—such as your dating life, finances, or career—from the Holy Spirit's control? If so, what tangible steps will you take this week to submit that area to the Holy Spirit? Remember, any part of your life that is not under the control of the Holy Spirit is open to demonic influence.

6. According to 1 John 2:1, what role does Jesus play whenever Satan levels an accusation against Christians? How does this affect your view of the spiritual battle you are a part of?

7. Read Colossians 1:13–14. Write out a prayer in the space provided, thanking God for rescuing you from the domain of darkness and transferring you to His kingdom of light through Jesus Christ.

Optional Activities

1. Do a topical study on angels in the Bible by using a concordance and cross-references. (You can also search "angel" and "angels" on biblegateway.com, blueletterbible.org, or similar websites.) After reading several verses, write out what you learned about angels.

2. Read 2 Kings 6:15–17. What do you learn about angels from this passage? What do you think you could see if your eyes were opened to the spiritual realm all around you?

Prayer Focus

Thank God for creating the angels, who communicate His messages and minister to us. Ask Him to help you be aware that your struggles in this life are not against flesh and blood but against spiritual forces. Examine your motives, aims, and priorities, and confess to Him any area that you have not fully submitted to the control of the Holy Spirit.

Assignment

1. Memorize Ephesians 6:12: "For our struggle is not against flesh and blood, but against the rulers, against the powers, against the world forces of this darkness, against the spiritual forces of wickedness in the heavenly places."

2. Read chapter 6 of the *What Every Christian Should Know* book and work through the corresponding study.

6

HUMANITY AND SIN

Session Topic: What was God's original plan for His human creation? Why did God give us free will? How does sin affect our relationship with God? This chapter shows us how to reclaim what God originally intended for us.

Icebreakers (Choose One)

1. The author said, "Today, we often use the word *human* as a catch-all defense for our worst instincts." What are some examples you've heard (or said) defending certain actions as "only human" or "human nature"?

2. If you asked the average person in our society, "Are you a good person?" how do you think he or she would respond? Why?

Group Discovery Questions

1. When God created humans, why didn't He just program us, like robots, to worship Him? What is the purpose of free will?

2. What does it mean to "glorify" God? (Look up *glorify* in a dictionary if that would be helpful.) How can we glorify God in our daily lives? Be as specific as you can.

3. In the garden of Eden, Satan blinded Eve to God's blessings by getting her to fixate on God's lone restriction. In what ways does Satan continue to use variations of that same tactic with believers today?

4. According to Romans 5:12, when Adam sinned by defying God's clear command in the garden of Eden, what was the result for all humanity?

5. Read Isaiah 6:3–5. What does it mean to be *holy*? How is holiness different from simply "being good"?

6. Read Habakkuk 1:13. What can we learn about God from this verse?

7. The author said, "Understanding God's holiness gives us a sense of the distance our sin has created between us and Him." Read Romans 3:23 and Isaiah 59:2, and discuss some of the devastating effects of our sin.

Personal Application Questions

1. If someone asked you, "Do you think you are a good person?" how would you respond? Be honest, and explain your answer. How does your "goodness" compare to God's holiness?

2. Think of a time when you did something wrong and got caught. What was your natural reaction? Did you immediately confess, or did you try to cover up your sin by denying it, lying about it, hiding it, or blaming someone else? What does this kind of response reveal about the sin nature we all inherited from Adam and Eve?

3. Read Genesis 3:21. What did God do in response to Adam and Eve's sin? Why is this significant?

4. Based on what you learned in this chapter, what was the purpose of the system of sacrifices and offerings in the Old Testament law? Did these sacrifices actually remove sins? Why or why not?

5. "Did God really say . . . ?" With those four words, Satan is able to plant doubts without directly challenging God. Can you think of a time in your life when Satan tempted you to doubt God's Word? Describe what happened.

6. According to the author, "Jesus's death on the cross removed the penalty of our sin and destroyed the power of sin over us once and for all. But it didn't eliminate the presence of sin from our lives. The ultimate war is won, yet many battles remain." What are some of the ongoing battles with sin you have experienced (or are currently experiencing)? What practical steps can you take to seek God's help in these battles?

7. Have you ever felt far away from God because of something you've done? Describe what happened. Then read Isaiah 44:22. What comfort do you gain from this verse?

Optional Activities

1. Choose one of the ongoing spiritual battles you mentioned in question #6 above, and use a concordance or Bible website (or ask another group member) to find Bible verses related to that issue. Write one of the verses on a note card and place it somewhere you will see it regularly to help you confront Satan's temptations with God's Word this week.

2. Break into groups of two or three, and consider the author's suggestions for our spiritual defense against Satan:

   - "Studying Scripture in a purposeful way, seeking answers to difficult questions and working to understand why we believe what we do."
   - "Spending time in prayer, asking God to reveal more truths from His Word."
   - "Talking with church leaders and mature believers, drawing from their wisdom on difficult topics."
   - "Engaging with people who don't necessarily share our views of God and Scripture, trying to answer their questions and respond to their objections."
   - "Finding accountability partners who will challenge us when they see things in our lives that need to be brought to our attention."

In what ways are you currently practicing each of these areas of spiritual defense? What areas, if any, do you need to improve in your ongoing struggle with your sin nature? Discuss practical ways to apply these strategies in your lives this week.

Prayer Focus

Praise God for His holiness. Thank Him for demonstrating His love for you by His provision of Jesus Christ, whose sacrifice on the cross paid the penalty you deserve for your sin. Confess any sins in your life, and thank Him for His forgiveness through Christ. Commit to seeking His Word, His will, and His presence as you strive to walk faithfully with Him.

Assignment

1. At the end of one day this week, reflect on your day and record on a piece of paper all your thoughts, attitudes, and actions (including things you did *not* do) that were not holy or glorifying to God. Be honest with yourself without making excuses. As you review your list, what realizations do you have about your own sinfulness? Confess your sins to God in prayer. Next, draw a large cross over the list, representing that Jesus died for those sins, and throw the paper away. Thank God for forgiving your sins through the once-and-for-all sacrifice of Jesus Christ.

2. Read chapter 7 of the *What Every Christian Should Know* book and work through the corresponding study.

7

SALVATION

Session Topic: Why do we need to be saved? Why did God demand a perfect sacrifice for sin? How should we respond to people who say it's intolerant to claim that there is only one way to heaven? This chapter helps us grasp the difficult issue of exclusivity that lies at the heart of God's plan of salvation.

Icebreakers (Choose One)

1. What do you think it means to be tolerant? How has our culture's definition of *tolerance* changed during the past few generations? Discuss a few examples.

2. Is there anyone you would be willing to die for? If so, why would you be willing to die for that person (or people)? Why would it be hard to die for someone who is your enemy?

Group Discovery Questions

1. Read Exodus 20:1–3. What did God say about Himself in these verses? What command did He give His people?

2. Read Genesis 6:14–16. Why do you think God specified such exact details for building the ark, as well as other commands in the Old Testament, such as constructing the temple and offering sacrifices? What do you think would have happened if Noah and the people hadn't followed God's specific instructions?

3. What did you learn from this chapter about the "way of Cain"? Read Genesis 4:2–5, Hebrews 11:4, and Jude 11 for more insight about the consequences of trying to approach God on our terms rather than on His terms.

4. Many people today say, "If you claim that Jesus is the only path to God, you're being intolerant." Is that true? Why or why not?

5. What did Jesus say about the way to heaven in Matthew 7:13–14? According to Jesus, will most people spend eternity in heaven or in hell? In verse 21, what did Jesus say is necessary for a person to enter heaven?

6. Has somebody ever said to you, "All religions teach basically the same thing"? If so, share your experience. After reading this chapter, how might you respond differently?

7. Discuss the author's statement: "Whenever God sees a heart that wants to know Him, He will send His truth into that person's life." How does this help answer the objection, "What about people who have never heard of Jesus?" (For more insight on this, see Acts 8:26–39 and Romans 1:18–20.)

Personal Application Questions

1. Read Romans 3:23 and Ephesians 2:1. What do you learn from these verses about your spiritual state apart from Jesus Christ?

2. Consider the author's statement: "Christianity is unique because it raises the performance requirements. Christianity doesn't say it's good enough to be good enough. Christianity says God's standard is absolute perfection." Read James 2:10 and write out what you learn about this high standard. How do you measure up to this standard?

3. According to Romans 6:23, what is the penalty for falling short of God's standard? What is God's free gift to you?

4. Read John 14:6, Acts 4:12, and Romans 10:9. Why is the exclusivity of Jesus Christ for salvation important in your life? How would your faith and your life be different if there were other ways to be saved?

5. The author listed four responses you can give when people object to the exclusivity of Jesus Christ for salvation:

- "Your argument is with the Bible, not with me."
- "God wants to save as many, not as few, people as possible."
- "The fact that God has provided one way of salvation demonstrates His love, not His hatred."
- "Consider the cost."

Which of these responses was most striking to you? Look up Bible verses to support that reasoning.

6. The author said, "We have an urgent message to proclaim—a matter of eternal life and death." What, if anything, is holding you back from sharing the message of salvation with the people around you? Ask God to help you overcome those obstacles.

7. Read Jesus's anguished plea to His heavenly Father in Matthew 26:39. If all roads lead to God—indeed, if *any* other road leads to God—that means Jesus's sacrifice wasn't necessary. In your own words, write out the unimaginable cost of salvation.

Optional Activities

1. Break into pairs, and role-play sharing the gospel of salvation with one another. Consider addressing the common objections to exclusivity discussed in this chapter.

2. The biggest decision you will ever make is whether you want to pay for your own sins or whether you will accept God's payment for your sins through Jesus Christ. If you would like to become a Christian and know for sure that one day you will be welcomed into heaven, I invite you to pray this prayer, knowing that God is listening:

> *Dear God,*
> *Thank You for loving me. I realize I have failed You in so many ways. And I am truly sorry for the sin in my life. I believe that You love me so much that You sent Your Son, Jesus, to die on the cross for me and take the punishment that I deserve for my sins. And right now, I am trusting in what Jesus did for me—not in my good works—to save me from my sins. Thank You for forgiving me. Help me to spend the rest of my life serving You. In Jesus's name, amen.*

Prayer Focus

Thank God for sending His only Son, Jesus Christ, to come to earth, live a sinless life, be crucified, and rise from the dead so that you could become the righteousness of God in Him. Confess your sins to Him, and thank God for His forgiveness through Jesus Christ. Ask God to give you opportunities to share the gospel with others this week.

Assignment

1. Memorize John 14:6: "I am the way, and the truth, and the life; no one comes to the Father but through Me."

2. Read chapter 8 of the *What Every Christian Should Know* book and work through the corresponding study.

8

THE CHURCH

Session Topic: Why is worship important in our relationship with God? How does fellowship with other Christians affect our spiritual health? What does it mean to be part of the body of Christ? This chapter reveals the vital role the church plays in our lives—and the vital role we play in the church.

Icebreakers (Choose One)

1. Share stories of times when someone from your church helped you or encouraged you in some way, such as through instruction, prayer, support, or perhaps even meeting a tangible need.

2. What are some reasons you chose to join (or participate in) your current church? Share with the group specific things you appreciate about your congregation.

Group Discovery Questions

1. Discuss the author's statement: "We cannot experience the Spirit's full power in our lives without being connected to a local church. After all, the church is the body of Christ, and each of us is a member of that body (1 Cor. 12:27)." Do you agree or disagree? Explain your answer.

2. Read Acts 2:1–8. What happened on the day of Pentecost? Why do you think the early church was given the supernatural ability to speak in foreign languages that day?

3. Read the spiritual gifts mentioned in 1 Corinthians 12:4–11, Romans 12:6–8, and Ephesians 4:11–12. How do you see these gifts being used in your church?

4. Read 2 Corinthians 11:9 and Philippians 4:15. In what ways can believers' financial gifts, such as tithes and offerings, help fellow believers and advance the ministry of the

church? How could tithing and giving offerings also help us grow spiritually?

5. What's the difference between uniformity and unity? Which one is the church called to, and why?

6. Read Psalm 34:3. Why is corporate worship (worshiping God together with other Christians) important to our spiritual health?

7. Read Ephesians 4:11–13. What do you learn from this passage about God's plan for the church?

Personal Application Questions

1. Are you currently a member of a local church? Why or why not? What did you learn from this chapter about the importance of church membership?

2. In what ways are you using your spiritual gift in the local church to serve the body of Christ? If you aren't currently using your spiritual gift, what step(s) will you take this week to begin exercising your God-given gift in the church? (If you aren't sure of your spiritual gift, ask your study group members what they think your gift might be.)

3. How do you prepare for corporate worship with your church? What changes, if any, would you like to make in your preparation for worshiping God with other believers?

4. Consider this statement from the author: "A personal study of God's Word is no substitute for sitting under the preaching of God's Word. There are more commands in the New Testament to listen to the Word of God from a sound teacher than there are to study the Word for yourself." What

preacher or Bible teacher do you listen to regularly? How does this person's teaching influence your spiritual growth?

5. Read Acts 2:42–46. What are some benefits, both to other believers and to you personally, of Christian fellowship? In what ways are you involved in the lives of fellow believers in your church? Is there anything you would like to improve in this area?

6. Read Acts 2:47. Why is sharing the gospel an essential ministry of the church? In what ways are you participating with your church in taking the gospel to unbelievers?

7. Read Matthew 6:19–21, then ask yourself, "How much can I give and invest in God's kingdom?" Spend some time in prayer asking God to show you how He wants you to invest the time, opportunities, and financial resources He has entrusted to you. Then write out your commitment in the space below.

Optional Activities

1. Think of someone in your church you can encourage or help in a tangible way this week. Make a plan and follow through to show God's love to that person or family.

2. Write an encouraging email or note to a pastor, staff member, or church member who has influenced you in some way. Be sure to thank him or her for helping you, and express your commitment to pray for that person.

Prayer Focus

Thank God for creating the church as a place for believers to enjoy worship, instruction, nourishment, and sharing. Ask Him to show you how you can become more involved in your church, using your spiritual gift to strengthen other believers.

Assignment

1. Memorize Hebrews 10:24–25: "Let us consider how to stimulate one another to love and good deeds, not forsaking our own assembling together, as is the habit of some, but encouraging one another; and all the more as you see the day drawing near."

2. Read chapter 9 of the *What Every Christian Should Know* book and work through the corresponding study.

FUTURE THINGS

Session Topic: How should we interpret biblical prophecies about the future? What difference do these prophecies make in our daily walk with Christ? When will God judge evil once and for all? This chapter reveals God's final plan for the world and offers a glimpse of what awaits us in eternity.

Icebreakers (Choose One)

1. Are you the kind of person who likes to read spoilers for movies or TV shows? Why or why not?

2. How would you rate your current understanding of biblical prophecy on a scale of 1 to 10, with 1 being "I have no idea" and 10 being "I completely understand everything the Bible teaches about the end times"?

Group Discovery Questions

1. What are some reasons Christians should study and understand biblical prophecy?

2. According to 2 Peter 3:11–18, what should a proper understanding of biblical prophecy motivate believers to do?

3. Read 1 Thessalonians 4:16–18. What can we learn from this passage about the rapture of the church?

4. Discuss the author's statement: "Perhaps the most pertinent aspect of the rapture is its imminence. There are no prophecies that must take place before it can occur. In short, the rapture can happen at any moment." How should the imminence of the rapture affect our daily lives as believers?

5. Read 2 Corinthians 5:9–10. What is the judgment seat of Christ? What is the purpose of this judgment? (See also 1 Corinthians 3:10–15.) In what ways is the judgment seat of Christ different from the great white throne judgment of unbelievers, described in Revelation 20:11–15?

6. Revelation 19:11–16 describes the second coming of Jesus Christ. How does this passage affect your perception of Jesus?

7. Read Revelation 21:1–5. What can we learn from this passage about the forever future God has planned for those who trust in Jesus Christ?

Personal Application Questions

1. What is your attitude toward biblical prophecy? Do you tend to dismiss prophecy as confusing or irrelevant, or do you tend to make studying prophecy a priority? Explain your answer.

2. Read Titus 2:11–13. What does it mean to "live sensibly, righteously and godly in the present age, looking for the blessed hope" of Christ's appearing? Be as specific as you can.

3. According to 2 Peter 3:9, why has God delayed the end times and His final judgment of unbelievers so far? How does this make you feel?

4. What are some things you are looking forward to experiencing in heaven?

5. What question did the Philippian jailer ask in Acts 16:30? What was Paul and Silas's reply in verse 31? The author stated, "That's the message that should occupy our time as we await the final trumpet blast." In what ways are you actively engaged in sharing this message with others so they, too, can spend eternity in heaven?

6. Consider the author's statement: "The world only seems to be spinning into chaos. The reality is that nothing is beyond God's control. Evil only seems to be winning the day. The reality is that the season for evil is drawing to a close. When God's plan unfolds, evildoers will never again prosper at the expense of others. Good people will never again suffer. God will take care of everything, according to His perfect timing and His perfect plan." What perspective does this give you on a situation you may be struggling with right now?

7. Read John 16:33. What is Jesus's promise to you in this verse?

Optional Activities

1. Read Matthew 24:14. Think of a foreign missionary or international missions organization your group could support with prayer, and possibly also a financial gift, as a way to participate in preaching the gospel to all the nations before the end comes.

2. Make a list of unbelievers you know in your family, your workplace, your school, and your community. Ask God to give you opportunities to talk with them, and commit to sharing the gospel of salvation with them before it's too late.

Prayer Focus

Thank God that nothing in this world is beyond His control. Praise Him for taking care of everything in the future, according to His perfect timing and His perfect plan. Commit to growing in your understanding of biblical prophecy as you seek to be salt and light in our world (Matt. 5:13–16). Ask Him to help you spread the gospel to as many people as possible before the world is swept away by God's judgment.

Assignment

1. Memorize 2 Peter 3:11–12: "Since all these things are to be destroyed in this way, what sort of people ought you to be in holy conduct and godliness, looking for and hastening the coming day of God."

2. Read chapter 10 of the *What Every Christian Should Know* book and work through the corresponding study.

10

CHRISTLIKENESS

Session Topic: What is God's plan for our lives? What role does the Holy Spirit play in helping us say no to sin? How can we develop the attitudes and characteristics of Christ? This chapter provides practical strategies to become more like Christ and live in freedom and victory.

Icebreakers (Choose One)

1. Describe someone you consider to be Christlike. What are some attitudes and actions of that person that remind you of Christ?

2. Who was your role model growing up—perhaps a parent, teacher, coach, sports figure, or another accomplished person? Describe why you chose that person as a role model. In what ways do you think your life could be different if you chose Jesus Christ as your role model now?

Group Discovery Questions

1. What does it mean to be Christlike? Do you think a Christian can truly become like Christ in this life? Explain your answer.

2. Look up *sanctification* in a dictionary and write out the definition in the space provided.

3. Read Philippians 1:6, Ephesians 4:22–24, and Colossians 3:8–14. According to these verses, is our sanctification God's responsibility, our responsibility, or both? Explain your answer.

4. Read Matthew 5:16 and Ephesians 2:8–10. If our good works can't save us, what role do they play in our lives as Christians?

5. According to 2 Peter 1:3, what has God given us? How do we access that power?

6. Discuss the author's statement about our struggle with sin: "The struggle gets easier the more often we choose to be controlled by the Holy Spirit. Think of it as a habit we develop. The more often we say yes to the Spirit and no to sin, the easier it becomes the next time to say yes to the Spirit and no to sin." Do you agree or disagree? Explain your answer, sharing personal experiences if desired.

7. Read Jesus's prayer in John 17:14–18. How can Christians live in this world, with its responsibilities and temptations, without loving this world and being conformed to its values? Be as specific as you can.

Personal Application Questions

1. According to Romans 8:28–29, what is God's purpose for your life?

2. Consider the author's statement: "I've found it's not the easy things that tend to make me more like Jesus. It's those hard things, those sad things, those things that defy our human understanding that God uses to chisel away anything un-Christlike in my life." What difficult thing(s) has God used in your life to make you more like Christ? Describe what happened.

3. Can you relate to the conundrum Paul expressed in Romans 7:21–25? Give an example from your own life. According to verse 25, who can set you free from this struggle?

4. Read Romans 6:12–13. What are some practical ways you can refuse to "let sin reign in your mortal body" by present-ing your body parts (such as your eyes, tongue, feet, and

mind) "as instruments of righteousness to God" in your daily life? Give specific examples.

5. Read Colossians 3:1–2. What do these verses encourage you to do? In what area(s) of your life do you need to be more heavenly minded?

6. Which of the six characteristics of Jesus Christ discussed in this chapter (*compassion, kindness, humility, gentleness, patience*, and *love*) do you most want to improve in your life? Write a prayer asking God to strengthen you in that area.

7. Christlikeness is a continual process—one day, one decision at a time for the rest of your life. But the good news is that you can start now! One year from today, what would you like to be different about your spiritual life? What steps will you take to reach those goals?

Optional Activities

1. Keep a journal this week of situations in which you have the choice to be controlled by the Spirit or to give in to the temptation to sin. How did you respond to these situations? What, if anything, would you like to do differently next time? Ask God to help you become more like Christ in your daily life.

2. Sometime during this study, someone has demonstrated Christlikeness to you, perhaps someone in your group or in your church. Reach out to that person this week, thanking him or her for setting an example of Christlikeness for you to follow.

Prayer Focus

Thank God for using everything in your life to work together for His purpose: to make you just like Jesus. Ask Him to chisel away anything in your life that's not like Jesus Christ and to help you love the things Jesus loved, do the things Jesus did, and act the way Jesus acted in every situation.

ABOUT
DR. ROBERT JEFFRESS

Dr. Jeffress is senior pastor of the fifteen-thousand-member First Baptist Church, Dallas, Texas, and is a Fox News contributor. He is also an adjunct professor at Dallas Theological Seminary. He has made more than four thousand guest appearances on various radio and television programs and regularly appears on major mainstream media outlets, such as Fox News Channel's *Fox and Friends*, *Hannity*, *Fox News @ Night with Shannon Bream*, and *Justice with Judge Jeanine*, as well as ABC's *Good Morning America* and HBO's *Real Time with Bill Maher*.

Dr. Jeffress hosts a daily radio program, *Pathway to Victory*, that is heard nationwide on over one thousand stations in major markets such as Dallas–Fort Worth, New York City, Chicago, Los Angeles, Houston, Washington, DC, Philadelphia, San Francisco, Portland, and Seattle.

Dr. Jeffress also hosts a daily television program, *Pathway to Victory*, that can be seen Monday through Friday on the Trinity Broadcasting Network (TBN) and every Sunday on TBN, Daystar, and the TCT Network. *Pathway to Victory* also airs seven days a week on the Hillsong Channel. His television broadcast reaches 195 countries and is on 11,295 cable and satellite systems throughout the world.

Dr. Jeffress is the author of almost thirty books, including *Perfect Ending, Not All Roads Lead to Heaven, A Place Called Heaven, Choosing the Extraordinary Life, Courageous, Invincible,* and *18 Minutes with Jesus.*

Dr. Jeffress led his congregation in the completion of a $135 million re-creation of its downtown campus. The project is the largest in modern church history and serves as a "spiritual oasis" covering six blocks of downtown Dallas.

Dr. Jeffress graduated with a DMin from Southwestern Baptist Theological Seminary, a ThM from Dallas Theological Seminary, and a BS from Baylor University. In May 2010, he was awarded a Doctor of Divinity degree from Dallas Baptist University. In June 2011, Dr. Jeffress received the Distinguished Alumnus of the Year award from Southwestern Baptist Theological Seminary.

Dr. Jeffress and his wife, Amy, have two daughters and three grandchildren.

ABOUT
PATHWAY TO VICTORY

Established in 1996, *Pathway to Victory* serves as the broadcast ministry of Dr. Robert Jeffress and First Baptist Church of Dallas, Texas.

Pathway to Victory stands for truth and exists to pierce the darkness with the light of God's Word through the most effective media available, including television, radio, print, and digital media.

Through *Pathway to Victory*, Dr. Jeffress spreads the good news of Jesus Christ to lost and hurting people, confronts an ungodly culture with God's truth, and equips the saints to apply Scripture to their everyday lives. More than a thousand radio stations in the United States broadcast the daily radio program, while Daystar, Trinity Broadcasting Network, and other Christian television networks air *Pathway to Victory* both in the United States and internationally.

Our mission is to provide practical application of God's Word to everyday life through clear, biblical teaching. Our goal is to lead people to become obedient and reproducing disciples of Jesus Christ, as He commanded in Matthew 28:18–20. As our ministry continues to expand, we are confident the Lord will use *Pathway to Victory* to advance the mission statement of First Baptist Dallas: to transform the world with God's Word . . . one life at a time.